O, Terrible Angel

Michael R. Burch

ANCIENT CYPRESS PRESS
Fort Lauderdale

Ancient Cypress Press
Fort Lauderdale
Florida, USA
www.ancientcypresspress.com

Copyright © 2013 Ancient Cypress Press
Ancient Cypress Press® is a registered trademark.

All rights reserved—no part of this book may be reproduced in any form without permission in writing from the publisher, except by a reviewer who wishes to quote brief passages in connection with a review in a magazine or newspaper.

ISBN: 978-0-9889648-1-5

Cover art: "Beth," by Mary Rae

Acknowledgments

Grateful acknowledgment is made to the publications in which the poems below first appeared.

Anthologies and awards:

"Mother's Smile" placed first in the Penguin Books (UK) Valentine's Day Contest
"Mother's Smile" appeared in *Poems for Big Kids*
"The Desk" appeared in *A Bouquet of Poems*
"She Gathered Lilacs" appeared in *Captivating Poetry* and *Anthology of Contemporary American Poetry*

First publications by country and publisher:

Stremez (Greece): "Love Is Not Love"
Shabestaneh (Iran): "She Gathered Lilacs"
The Word (England): "Will There Be Starlight"
Nutty Stories (South Africa): "Because Her Heart Is Tender"
Grassroots Poetry (United States): "Will There Be Starlight"
Tucumcari Literary Review (United States): "Moments"
Writer's Journal (United States): "Once"
SP Quill (United States): "Melting"
Erosha (United States): "Warming Her Pearls"
mojo risin' magazine (United States): "Enigma"
Songs of Innocence (United States): "Virginal"
Poetic License/Monumental Moments (United States): "Are You the Thief" (as "Baring Pale Flesh")
The Eclectic Muse (Canada) "Because Her Heart Is Tender"

The Lyric (United States)
   "Once"
   "At Once"
   "Dawn"
The Neovictorian/Cochlea (United States)
   "Because Her Heart Is Tender"
   "Love Is Not Love"
   "She Gathered Lilacs"
Romantics Quarterly (United States)
   "Moments"
   "At Once"
   "She Spoke"
TALESetc (United States)
   "The Desk"
   "Mother's Smile"
   "A True Story"

Contents

Enigma	15
Because Her Heart Is Tender	16
Are You the Thief	17
Because You Came to Me	18
She Gathered Lilacs	19
Warming Her Pearls	20
Passionate One	21
Kissin' 'n' Buzzin'	22
Moments	23
She Spoke	24
Let Me Give Her Diamonds	25
Righteous	26
Will There Be Starlight?	27
Love Is Not Love	28
If	29
Virginal	30
The Quickening	31
The One True Poem	32
The Poem of Poems	33
The Last Defense of Love	34
Once	35
At Once	36
Gravity and Brilliance	37
Give and Take	38
Your Gift	39
Every Man Has a Dream	40

Oasis	41
It's Not Too Late	42
Melting	43
Afterglow	44
Love Is Her Belief and Her Commandment	45
Lightning	46
Sparks	47
Elemental	48
Wildest, Truest	49
All Her Sorrow	50
Flux	51
Kin	52
Grace	53
The Stand	54
For Nothing, All	55
Enchanted	56
Constant Forever	57
In Thrall	58
Entreaty	59
In Moments of Quietude, Love	60
Your Tender Warmth	61
Flesh Softer than Gold	62
tonight how i miss you	63
Her Absence	64
No Words, a Valentine	65
Becoming	66
Cameo	67
The Garden of Love	68

Dawn	69
Improvement on Shakespeare	70
What If We Had Never Met?	71
Is the Mirror Unkind?	72
Give Her All Stars	73
Incommunicado	74
Lines for Our Fourteenth Anniversary	75
Love Is the Strongest Diamond	76
For Beth on Valentine's Day	77
She Is Brighter than Dawn	78
Incense	79
For Our Wedding Night	80
Bed Head	81
Piddiless	82
Love If It Were Fragile	84
Honey in the Lion's Mouth	85
Beauty Within and Without	86
Pearl	87
A Sip from the Teacup	88
The Search	89
Love's Exemplar	90
My Angel	91
Your Heart's Rose (I)	92
Your Heart's Rose (II)	92
Beth's Advice to a Slowly Awakening World	93
My Epitaph	94
Requiem: Remember My Laughter	94
After the Deluge (I)	95

After the Deluge (II)	96
My Eve (I)	97
My Eve (II)	97
Love	98
Enigma (II)	99
Mother's Smile	100
The Desk	101
Reflex	102
Precipice	103
Success	104
Love's Extreme Unction	105
Boundless	106
Lullaby	107
A True Story	108
Always	109
Hushed, Yet Melodic	110
Passages on Fatherhood	111
The Watch	112
To My Child, Unborn	113
Transition	114
What Does It Mean?	115
With a Child's Wonder	116
About Michael R. Burch	119

O, Terrible Angel
for
Elizabeth Harris Burch

I wrote these poems for the love of my life: my beautiful, sweet, wonderful, captivating wife, Beth. Elizabeth is a noble—even a regal—name. Beth is also a sweet, gentle, tender name. They both suit her, because she combines the best attributes of nobility—courage, loyalty and a strong sense of justice—with a sweet, gentle tenderness. The "terrible" in my title above, and in the first line of this book's first poem, is "terrible" in the sense of "inspiring awe."

In his epiphany on Divine Love, the great Christian evangelist, Saint Paul, affirmed that Love is greater than either hope or faith, and that Love never gives up and never fails. But he also said that in this life we see through a glass, darkly. Plato said something similar when he spoke of earthly life being like a cave in which we see only shadows of the true, eternal, perfect forms. Mystics who have out-of-body experiences sometimes report visits to realms beyond suffering and death, that sound like heaven. And children who have near-death experiences often report following an attractive light—some call it the light of unconditional love—into the presence of God and the Angels, and what certainly sounds like heaven.

Perhaps the closest we come to a vision of heaven here on earth is the love of a good mother. If I was asked to explain this book's main theme, I would say that its main theme is Love, as personified in the form of a human angel, Beth. Until heaven is finally achieved, the world would do well to emulate her.

O, Terrible Angel

Enigma

O, terrible angel,
bright lover and avenger,
full of whimsical light
and vile anger;
wild stranger,
seeking the solace of night,
or the danger;
pale foreigner,
alien to man, or savior.

Who are you,
seeking consolation and passion
in the same breath,
screaming for pleasure, bereft
of all articles of faith,
finding life
harsher than death?

Grieving angel,
giving more than taking,
how lucky the man
who has found in your love,
this—our reclamation;
fallen wren,
you must strive to fly
though your heart is shaken;
weary pilgrim,
you must not give up
though your feet are aching;
lonely child,
lie here still in my arms;
you must soon be waking.

Because Her Heart Is Tender

She scrawled soft words in soap: "Never Forget,"
Dove-white on her car's window, and the wren,
because her heart is tender, might regret
it called the sun to wake her. As I slept,
she heard lost names recounted, one by one.

She wrote in sidewalk chalk: *"Never Forget,"*
and kept her heart's own counsel. No rain swept
away those words, no tear leaves them undone.

Because her heart is tender with regret,
bruised by razed towers' glass and steel and stone
that shatter on and on and on and on,
she stitches in damp linen: *"NEVER FORGET,"*
and listens to her heart's emphatic song.

The wren might tilt its head and sing along
because its heart once understood regret
when fledglings fell beyond, beyond, beyond ...
its reach, and still the boot-heeled world strode on.

She writes in adamant: *"NEVER FORGET,"*
because her heart is tender with regret.

Are You the Thief

When I touch you now,
O sweet lover,
full of fire,
melting like ice
in my embrace,
when I part the delicate white lace,
baring pale flesh,
and your face
is so close
that I breathe your breath
and your hair surrounds me like a wreath ...
tell me now,
O sweet, sweet lover,
in good faith:
are you the thief
who has stolen my heart?

Because You Came to Me

Because you came to me with sweet compassion
and kissed my furrowed brow and smoothed my hair,
I do not love you after any fashion,
but wildly, in despair.

Because you came to me in my black torment
and kissed me fiercely, blazing like the sun
upon parched desert dunes, till in dawn's foment
they melt, I am undone.

Because I am undone, you have remade me
as suns bring life, as brilliant rains endow
the earth below with leaves, where you now shade me
and bower me, somehow.

She Gathered Lilacs

She gathered lilacs
and arrayed them in her hair;
tonight, she taught the wind to be free.

She kept her secrets
in a silver locket;
her companions were starlight and mystery.

She danced all night
to the beat of her heart;
with her tears she imbued the sea.

She hid her despair
in a crystal jar,
and never revealed it to me.

She kept her distance
as though it were armor;
gauntlet thorns guard her heart like the rose.

*Love!—awaken, awaken
to see what you've taken
is still less than the due my heart owes!*

Warming Her Pearls

Warming her pearls, her breasts
gleam like constellations.
Her belly is a bit rotund ...
she might have stepped out of a Rubens.

Passionate One

Love of my life,
light of my morning,
arise brightly dawning,
for you are my sun.

Give me of heaven
both manna and leaven,
desirous Presence,
Passionate One.

Kissin' 'n' Buzzin'

Kissin' 'n' buzzin'
the bees rise
in a dizzy circle of two.
Oh, when I'm with you,
I feel like kissin' 'n' buzzin' too.

Moments

There were moments
full of promise,
like the petal-scented rainfall
of early spring,
when to hold you in my arms
and to kiss your willing lips
seemed everything.

There are moments
strangely empty
full of pale unearthly twilight
—how the cold stars stare!—
when to be without you
is a dark enchantment
the night and I share.

She Spoke

She spoke
and her words
were like a ringing echo dying
or like smoke
rising and drifting
while the earth below is spinning.

She awoke
with a cry
from a dream that had no ending,
without hope
or strength to rise,
into hopelessness descending.

And an ache
in her heart
toward that dream, retreating,
left a wake
of small waves
in circles never completing.

Let Me Give Her Diamonds

Let me give her diamonds
for my heart's
sharp edges.

Let me give her roses
for my soul's
thorn.

Let me give her solace
for my words
of treason.

Let the flowering of love
outlast a winter
season.

Let me give her books
for all my lack
of reason.

Let me give her candles
for my lack
of fire.

Let me kindle incense,
for our hearts
require

the breath-fanned
flaming perfume
of desire.

Righteous

Come to me tonight
in the twilight, O, and the full moon rising,
spectral and ancient, will mutter a prayer.

Gather your hair
and pin it up, knowing
that I will release it a moment anon.

We are not one,
nor is there a scripture
to sanctify nights you might spend in my arms,

but the swarms
of stars revolving above us
revel tonight, the most ardent of lovers.

Will There Be Starlight?

Will there be starlight
tonight
while she gathers
damask
and lilac
and sweet-scented heathers?

And will she find flowers,
or will she find thorns
guarding the petals
of roses unborn?

Oh, will there be moonlight
tonight
while she gathers
seashells
and mussels
and albatross feathers?

And will she find treasure
or will she find pain
at the end of this rainbow
of moonlight on rain?

Love Is Not Love

Love is not love that never looked
within itself and questioned all,
curled up like a zygote in a ball,
throbbed, sobbed and shook.

(Or went on a binge at a nearby mall,
and would not cook.)

Love is not love that never winced,
then smiled, convinced
that soar's the prerequisite of fall.

When all
its wounds and scars have been saline-rinsed,
where does Love find the wherewithal
to try again,
endeavor, when

all that it knows
is: *O, because!*

If

If I regret
fire in the sunset
exploding on the horizon,
then let me regret loving you.

If I forget
even for a moment
that you are the only one,
then let me forget that the sky is blue.

If I should yearn
in a season of discontentment
for the vagabond light of a companionless moon,
let dawn remind me that you are my sun.

If I should burn—one moment less brightly,
one moment less true—
then with wild scorching kisses,
inflame me, inflame me, inflame me anew.

Virginal, for Elizabeth

For an hour
every wildflower
beseeches her,
"To thy breast,
Elizabeth."

But she is mine;
her lips divine
and her breasts and hair
are mine alone.
Let the wildflowers moan.

The Quickening

I never meant to love you
when I held you in my arms
promising you sagely
wise, noncommittal charms.

And I never meant to need you
when I touched your tender lips
with kisses that intrigued my own—
such kisses I had never known,
nor a heartbeat in my fingertips!

The One True Poem

love was not meaningless,
nor your embrace, nor your kiss ...

and though every god proved a phantom,
still You were divine to your last dying atom ...

so that when You are gone
and, yea, not a word remains of this poem,

even so,
We were One.

The Poem of Poems

This is my Poem of Poems, for you.
Every word ineluctably true:
I love you.

The Last Defense of Love

... if all the parables of Love
fell mute, and every sermon too,
and every hymn and votive psalm
proved insufficient to the task
of proving Love might yet be true
in such a cruel, uncaring world ...
the last defense of Love, my Love,
the gods might offer, would be You.

Once

Once when her kisses were fire incarnate
and left in their imprint bright lipstick, and flame;
when her breath rose and fell over smoldering dunes,
leaving me listlessly sighing her name ...

Once when her breasts were as pale, as beguiling,
as wan rivers of sand shedding heat like a mist,
when her words would at times softly, mildly rebuke me
all the while as her lips did more wildly insist ...

Once when the thought of her echoed and whispered
through vast wastelands of need like a Bedouin chant,
I ached for the touch of her lips with such longing
that I vowed all my former vows to recant ...

Once, only once, something bloomed, of a desiccate seed—
this implausible blossom her wild rains of kisses decreed.

At Once

Though she was fair,
though she sent me the epistle of her love at once
and inscribed therein love's antique prayer,
I did not love her at once.

Though she would dare
pain's pale, clinging shadows, to approach me at once,
the dark, haggard keeper of the lair,
I did not love her at once.

Though she would share
the all of her being, to heal me at once,
yet more than her touch I was unable bear.
I did not love her at once.

And yet she would care,
and pour out her essence ...
and yet—there was more!
I awoke from long darkness
and yet—she was there.
I loved her the longer;
I loved her the more
because I did not love her at once.

Gravity and Brilliance

Night, and the earth
careers through the Void ...
Life is created.
Life is destroyed.
Those gone before us
observe from faint stars ...
God keeps his silence.
Old edicts lose force.
Only your love
remains steadfast and true ...
your gravity and brilliance
warm, center, renew.

Give and Take

Give her the stars and she'll ask for the moon's
cryptic rune.
Give her June's moon and she'll bargain for the sun
come late autumn.
But tell her you need her when the icicles splinter
and she'll gladly give you all her dear warmth
every winter.

Your Gift

Counsel, console.
This is your gift.

Calm, kiss and encourage.
Tenderly lift
each world-wounded heart
from its near-fatal dart.

Wise, mend every rift.

Bid pain, "Depart!"
Help friends' healing to start.
Keep every reason to grieve
for your own untaught heart.

Every Man Has a Dream

Every man has a dream that he cannot quite touch ...
a dream of contentment, of soft, starlit rain,
of a breeze in the evening that, rising again,
reminds him of something that cannot have been,
and he calls this dream Love.

And each man has a dream that he fears to let live,
for he knows that to hope is to throw away all,
so he curses, denies it and locks it within
the cells of his heart and he calls it a sin,
this madness, this Love.

But each man in his living falls prey to his dreams,
and he struggles, but so he ensures that he falls,
and he finds in the end that he cannot deny
the hope that he feels or the tears that he cries
in the darkness of night for this light he calls Love.

Oasis

I want tears to form again
in the shriveled glands of these eyes
dried all these long years
by too much heated knowing.

I want tears to course down
these parched cheeks,
to star these cracked lips
like an improbable dew
in the heart of a desert.

I want words to burble up
like happiness, like the thought of love,
like the overwhelming, shimmering thought of you
to a nomad who
has only known drought.

It's Not Too Late

It's not too late to sing of love, to sing
of beauty, though the moonless night obscures
each thing of sprawling loveliness that clings
to life in nettled darkness, and endures.

It's not too late to think of dawn, to think
of brightness on the water, of your face
unguarded at the moment planets sink
beneath some dim horizon, into Space.

It's not too soon to dream of night, to dream
of sleeping to your breasts' soft pantomime
of earth's own breathing sleep, of hills that climb
and dip, and taste of lilac and jasmine.

Melting

Entirely, as spring consumes the snow,
the thought of you consumes me: I am found
in rivulets, dissolved to what I know
of former winters' passions. Underground,
perhaps one slender icicle remains
of what I was before, in some dark cave—
a stalactite, long calcified, now drains
to sodden pools, whose milky liquid laves
the colder rock, thus washing something clean
that never saw the light, that never knew
the crust could break above, that light could stream:
so luminous,
        so bright,
                so beautiful ...
I lie revealed, and so I stand transformed,
and all because you smiled on me, and warmed.

Afterglow

The night is full of stars—which ones exist?
A trillion years from now, perhaps we'll know.
For now, I hold your wan hands to my lips,
your living hands—warm, capable and slow ...
so slow to feel this reckless night in me,
this moon in ceaseless orbit I became,
compelled by stranger gravity to flee
night's universe of suns, for one pale flame ...
for one pale flame that seemed to signify
the Zodiac of all, the meaning of
man's wandering flight past aimlessness. To lie
in dawning recognition is enough ...
enough each night to bask in you, to know
the face of Love ... eyes closed ... its afterglow.

Love Is Her Belief and Her Commandment

Love is her belief and her commandment;
in restless dreams at night, she dreams of Love;
and Love is her desire and her purpose;
and everywhere she goes, she sings of Love.

There is a tomb in Palestine: for others
the chance to stake their claims (the Chosen Ones),
but in her eyes it's Love's most hallowed chancel
where Love was resurrected, where one comes
in wondering awe to dream of resurrection
to blissful realms, where Love reigns over all
with tenderness, with infinite affection.

While some may mock her faith, still others wonder
because they see the rare state of her soul,
and there are rumors: when she prays the heavens
illume more brightly, as if saints concur
who keep a constant vigil over her.

And once she prayed beside a dying woman:
the heavens opened and the angels came
revealed as long-departed friends and loved ones,
to comfort and encourage. *I believe
not in her God, but always in her Love.*

Lightning

There are times before the appearance of the comet
when the course of a life is set,
then we enter into the moment.

Skies of blue, skies of slate, skies of ecstatic violet and jet—
the times to come, the moments we expected to share ...
were merely potential then. Still, the very air

was charged with possibilities, as though
lightning lurked beyond the horizon, in obscure and distant
skies ...
and then I looked into your sparking eyes.

Sparks

Unto the night
with its moon bright-ascending,
I whisper your name
and the shimmering rain
pauses, then ceases descending.

Who are you child?
The owl also wonders,
and the heavy-lidded sky,
with its bizarre lightnings and thunders ...
and still more exciting, the electricity the thought of you
conjures.

Elemental

There is within her a welling forth
of Love unfathomable.
She is not comfortable
with the thought of merely loving:
but she must give all.

At night, she heeds the storm's calamitous call.
Nay, longs for it. Why?
O, if a man understood, he might understand her.
But that would never do!

Beth, as you embrace the storm,
so I embrace elemental you.

Wildest, Truest

Hers is the wildest heart,
though increasingly tame,
like a thunderstorm
becoming rain.

Hers is the truest heart
I'll ever know:
an immaculate expanse
of virgin snow.

All Her Sorrow

All her sorrow,
never borne lightly
but contemplated nightly,
accumulates
to an almost infinite mass.
She is weary,
prone to eerie
haunting dreams.
And now it seems
her tears grow heavy
till no levee
can withstand,
nor any man.

Flux

You were like sunshine and rain—
begetting rainbows,
full of contradictions, like the intervals
between light and shadow.

That within you which I most opposed
drew me closer still,
as a magnet exerts its unyielding pull
on insensate steel.

Kin

O pale, austere moon,
haughty beauty,

what do we know of love,
or duty?

Grace

I did not squander my light
but kept in it a place
of pure human embrace.

Now "saints" might cry *Disgrace!*
because I touched your breast,
as if I'd failed some test

but I would say *more blessed*
because you kissed my face.

The Stand

Love is the end of all endeavor—
the perfect work no hand
can do, or undo ... the Stand
we take against Forever.

For Nothing, All

For nothing more than a moonlit night
and a few trillion stars
strewn about like so much silver dust ...

for nothing save the wine, the candlelight
and your heady perfume, sedulous as must,
and your eyes so full of trust,

I fell in love.

Enchanted

Sleep tight;
the earth's delight
is not the dawn,

but this disbelieving finger,
able to linger
such lips upon.

Constant Forever

She is all sweetness and light,
and about her there is the fragrance
of roses, and the vagrance
of love is in her eyes.

Still, when she cries,
when she is weary, though her heart is true,
she despairs every cloud, bids the sky to be blue
every day ...

for that is her way.
And, no, I would never change her,
be cruel to her, no, nor a stranger,
but as she is to me, so let me stay:

constant forever.

In Thrall

Tonight I have come
to the wrong conclusion
again, and I know—
love's a strange transfusion
of perilous liquids
and traitorous breath
embezzled from gods
to the laughter of Death.

Thus the bastard exists—
pale Mortality, born
like the frail-petalled rose
to adorn
some Dark Thorn.

And I know this, and yet
I know nothing at all ...
but Love's frail-petalled breath
and the sweet wherewithal
of your lips, mine in thrall ...

Thus, I taste crushing sweetness
where I ought to taste gall.

Entreaty

Her heart has borne too much sadness,
an overwhelming weight, the heaviness
of learning too soon of the emptiness
of being alone.

Now we are one,
but caught up sometimes in our differences,
forgetting the balm of a sweet caress,
our arguments border on heartlessness.

Yet I love her so.
Beth, oh my darling, please don't go ...

My life without you would be meaningless
and my love without you become nothingness
and my dreams without you would be naught, or less.

Do not make it so.

In Moments of Quietude, Love

In moments of quietude, Love
becomes far more than even the finest balm or ointment,
healing our world and holding our lives together
while warming and containing our orbits
and suddenly I am reminded of
the sun on a sunny morning
when all the flowers lifting their weary heads
begin to magically stir and brighten
so that, at that moment, life seems ordained
and with it, us—not only as observers
but also as creatures like those fantastical bottom-dwellers
who evolved to create their own Light.

Your Tender Warmth

Feelings deepen.
Nights lengthen.
The moon grows paler.
Winds strengthen.

But your sweet warmth
will never fail
though the stars expire
in a black gale.

And the mystics say
true love will prevail
at the end of time
though our vision is frail.

So hold me tight;—
Love, come, share with me
the tender warmth
of eternity.

Flesh Softer than Gold

For all that is lost,
still something remains—
this moment we shared—
this sadness, this joy.
And who knows the cost
of Love's brief alloy?
Many mothers have dared
birth's wild-wrenching pains—
delighting to hold
flesh softer than gold.

Love is not wisdom
and yes, life holds terror.
Perhaps God's in error.
Perhaps man's a bust.
But one thing I trust—
you, my Love, were no error.
So I'll brave every terror—
to have and to hold
your flesh softer than gold.

tonight how i miss you

tonight how i miss You, as never before,
though morning is only a moment away.
o, i know i should sleep, but i lie here, distraught,
as You flit through my mind—such a wild, haunting
Thought.

and Love is a dream that i lately imagined—
a dream, yet so real i can touch it at times.
but how to explain? i can hardly envision
my self without You, like a farce without mimes.

deep, deep in my soul lurks a creature of fire,
dormant, not living unless You are near;
now, because You are gone, he grows dim, and in dire
need of your Presence, he wavers, i fear ...

how he and i wish, how we wish you were here.

Her Absence

When she is gone,
when she is far away,
when day is done,
when she is not there to say
that she loves me,
when morning seems far away
and darkness looms like a sea
stretching out endlessly
between night and day,
sometimes I dream her near
though sleep remains elusive, so far away,
and I say ...
I tell her how much I love her
thinking she might appear ...
but the sky only grows the more gray ...

No Words, a Valentine

What use are words when the neophyte "teaches"?
Who needs a Muse, when True Love holds the floor?
There are no words for this heart that now reaches,
  with each tender passage, to say even more.

There are no jewels as bright as your laughter,
nor one precious diamond worth one of your tears;
there are no moments, none now, nor hereafter
  sweeter or better than those with your near.

There is no woman I ever held dearer,
nor longed so to call both my friend and my bride.
Which wanton, which angel could lure me the nearer?
  (And since you are both, I need never decide).

There is no hearth as warm as your laughter;
  there are no kisses (none!) half as divine
  as your gentle kisses (before, during, after)
the hours when the sun and your clothing decline.

Becoming

A willowy yew thrust out its shoots
through all the long decades
of defiant rains ...

till, silhouetted in a winter mist,
ice-shagged and -barnacled,
it sagged and groaned.

Ecstatic feet no longer strayed
within its eerie borders; so it knew
a kind of peace.

Though overgrown
with stiff brown moss,
it did not care,

awaiting,
in the chalcedonic silence there,
the pale catharsis of that face:

that face, that Face,—
the very countenance and sum
of all that it had reached for,

and become.

Cameo

Through the years,
though sometimes softened by tears,
we endured.

Endured,
and yet your loving heart
did not grow hard
(no, not a thing of sard!)
but, oh, in your palest cameo
the shape of your heart
emerged.

*

This was your starring role,
you whose transcendent heart
needed no marquee,
only a child to love,
and me,
and an ever-expanding world
of friends, loves and family.

*

Now this is your starring role:
your heart the centerpiece
and your magnificent soul,
loving and giving at ease,
once a tender and wounded soul,
now delighted and willing to please.

You won! You claimed victory
over the brutal world
fair angel, sweet mother! (Wild girl!)

The Garden of Love

Love came to me
in an unreasonable season
for an unseasonable reason,
as Love always does ...

like a late-blooming rose
in a wasteland of briars
tended palely by friars
singing chastity's laws
(but Love smiled, because
She's above all men's flaws).

Then Love sent the rose
the sweet warmth of your face,
the bright rains of your grace
in Her mysterious cause ...

and thus hope has bloomed
in a heart once thought doomed.

Dawn
for Beth and Laura

Bring your nuclear power
to the strange nightmarish fray:
wrap up your cherished ones
in the golden light of day.

Improvement on Shakespeare

I'd make her immortal
but her love beat me to it.
Still, at least I can chortle:
"I was wise, 'cause I knew it."

What If We Had Never Met?

What if we had never met;
had never fumbled with the fragility of love;
had never swallowed the bittergreen taste of regret;
had never choked on the ash of remorse;
had never smiled, groped and swept
a disgruntled remark under the carpet
like a cheap cigarette?

What if we had never kept
the secret expectation of other lives
in secluded compartments like knives
tarnished with unuse,
although they had been meant to slice
our hearts open like grapefruit?

What it our love had not gone a little sour at times,
like a dour vinegar extracted from wine,
beneficial only for its astringency?

What if we had never met? ...

What if we had never met?
How could I not have loved you,
have not have planted the seed of our son deep within you
in the waterfall course of your expectation
of a light so bright I could not comprehend,
but stood blind,
overwhelmed,
drowning in radiance?

What if we had never met?

Is the Mirror Unkind?

To your lovely brown eyes is the mirror unkind,
revealing far more than reflections defined
in superficial glass, so lacking in depth?
Is the mirror unkind, at times, darling Beth?

What you see, my dear, I see different by far,
as our sun from Centauri is just a "small" star,
but here it brings life and warms each day's start.
Oh, and a mirror can never reveal a true heart.

Give Her All Stars

Gather up Sparks from the hearth of the heavens;
give her all Stars to heighten her eyes;
give her the Moon or some vagabond Planet;
give her the Wind, the communion of sighs.

Tell her the tale of a butterfly princess
climbing to heaven on gossamer wings,
or sing her sweet songs of the last true enchantment:
the wild, plaintive song the sad nightingale sings.

Or favor her heart with a white incantation;
let unicorns bear her to Aasgard above ...
none of these mysteries are mine, alas!, to give her,
but that which I have I will give her—my love.

Incommunicado

I do not deserve her,
nor can I give her what she deserves:
all the sweet and gently-rendered love words
(a failing all too common in a man).

If I could, I would tell her
that her kindness has touched me in so many ways,
that the light of her presence has brightened my days,
and that I love her.

If I knew how, I would show her
that her Love has become the sweet-beckoning light
illuminating my path through the darkest night,
like a radiant meteor shower.

If I could tell her.

Lines for Our Fourteenth Anniversary

Beth is the gentlest name I know—
as light on the tongue as a flake of snow.

It seems the name a child might teach
soft things that fall within his reach,
like autumn leaves, the art of speech.

It's bruised, sometimes, like purple petals
sequestered by cruel, sharp-spined nettles.

It's cloudy, like the voice of kettles
crooning softly to themselves.
It's curious, like the songs of elves.

Oh, Beth is the tenderest name I know—
as light as the sound of the deepening snow.

Love Is the Strongest Diamond

Love is the strongest diamond,
though it's never hardened by time.

No weight can ever crush it;
it only grows more sublime.

Though we lie in our graves, my darling,
we need fear no ultimate crime

for our love cannot be stolen,
as long as your heart is mine.

This diamond is merely a token
of our love: precious, bright and unbroken.

This diamond, and also this rhyme.

For Beth, on Valentine's Day

I could not find a gift as rare,
as sweetly scented as your hair,
though fields of fragrant lilacs bloom
exquisite, delicate and fair.

I could not hope to find a prize
as captivating as your eyes,
though crystal shackles light within
its ambient device.

I thought to give a gift of words;
they came, then fled like flitting birds,
till I was left alone again
with lines of pale and palsied verse.

But let me wish you on this day
a life resplendent, marvelous, gay …
and let me wish for you each night
peace, dreams and stars in wild array.

And may God's peace, the whitest dove,
smile down on you from high above.
For one who has so many gifts,
accept one more—this poem, with love.

She Is Brighter than Dawn

There's a light about her
like the moon through a mist:
a starry transcendence
with which she is blessed

and my heart to her light
like the tide now is pulled ...
she is fair, O, and bright
like the moon silver-veiled.

There's a fire within her
like the sun's leaping forth
to lap up the darkness
of night from earth's hearth

and my eyes to her flame
like a moth now are drawn
till my heart is consumed.
She is brighter than dawn.

Incense

To be so fair
where there is sorrow,
a light must shine.
Tonight, it shines.

Now, like a rose
that seeks the sun,
toward your light
my heart inclines.

To be so sweet
when life is bitter,
true Love must bloom.
O, what a Bloom!

Here at the altar,
my desirable Priestess,
my heart gives thanks
for such perfume.

For Our Wedding Night

Tonight, you will be a virgin to me,
for your heart is true
and your heart is pure
and these two virtues forever endure.

Tonight, you will be an angel to me,
for your face will glow
and your eyes will shine
with a Love both earthly and divine.

Tonight, you will be a wife to me:
the woman I want
the woman I take
to love forever, and never forsake.

Bed Head,
or
the Ballad of Beth and Her Fur Babies

When Beth and her babies
prepare for "good night"
sweet rituals of kisses
and cuddles commence.

First Wickett, the mensch
whose mane has grown light
with the wisdom of age
and advanced senescence
is tucked in, "just right."

Then Mary, the mother,
is smothered with kisses
in a way that befits
such an angelic missus.

Then Melody, lambkin,
and sweet, soulful Oz
and Zander the Clever
all clap their cool paws
and follow dear Beth
to their warm nightly roost
where they'll sleep on her head
(or, perhaps, her caboose).

Piddiless

Lines in which the Poet explains why his Piddies are off limits, even to Beth.

Love can be giddy;
love can be sad;
but Piddies fly solo
(so don't make them mad).
Love can be bought
or sometimes freely had,
but a Piddy cannot
(or it acts like a cad).

*All Piddies are loners;
all Piddies deny
any need to be cuddled
or tickled. (Don't try!)*

It's true that some lovers
think Piddies can change,
so they try to reform them
(they end up estranged).
'Cause Piddies are hermits
like the Unabomber:
antisocial types
who won't write their own momma!

*Yes, Piddies are loners
and Piddies deny
any need to be cuddled
or tickled. (Don't try!)*

So a word to the wise:
Your intentions? Abort them!
They're misogynists
so there's no need to court them.
A Piddy who's tickled
will lose all composure
and seek sweet revenge
as a cruel form of closure.

For all Piddies are loners,
so my Piddies deny
any need to be cuddled
or tickled. (Don't try!)

Love, If It Were Fragile

Love, if it were fragile,
would vanish like a puff of smoke in the wind,
but Love is not fragile,
and though we have lashed out, and though we have sinned
against each other,
still, I would have no other lover,
nor can I see myself waking in the morning without you:
how could that be?
How could I ever doubt you
or doubt your Love for me?

Emptiness and darkness gather around us
and the loss of hope sometimes confounds us
and our apathy and our despair may astound us,
and yet Love still can be,
still surrounds us.

How can Love not be?

Honey in the Lion's Mouth

"A swarm of bees had left honey in the lion's carcass."

... like the bitter scent of clover,
so the taste of Love is bitter,
perhaps a little sweeter
for the bounty, where flies hover ...

... in the lion's gaping maw,
see, the rich dark honey runs ...
*stranger proms and cummerbunds
and Love's strange, imperious law ...*

... yet so tender, like the thought
that if all this comes to naught
still we laughed and sipped, devout,
at the honeysuckle's spout ...

Beauty Within and Without

A beautiful day?
Well, yes then ... okay ...
But *you,* my dear darling?
Oh, my! My! Olé!

For there's something within you
the stars are without—
love, wisdom, desire, tenderness, doubt—
that makes me so bubbly inside that I say:
You, my sweet darling?
Oh, my! Hip-hooray!

A beautiful day? Quite true, I suppose ...
somewhere someone's praising a sun-dappled rose
while ignoring its thorns and sharp nettles nearby,
not to mention the compost that reeks like a sty!
So I (being wiser) will praise your sweet spirit,
your kindness, your Love ...
hope you don't cringe to hear it!
They make me so giddy inside that I say,
Oh, my beautiful darling!
Olé! Hip-hooray!

Pearl
for Beth, my pearl of inestimable worth

Her heart is transparent
or semi-opaque
like a lustrous pearl
given as a keepsake ...

and who knows the depths
at which it, sequestered,
fashioned moonbeams from tears
as grit-irritants festered ...

till a diver approached
and, with a wondering hand,
harvested Love,
bore it to his homeland ...

A Sip from the Teacup

Lines written after a dream in which I prayed to experience the love of God, then realized I had found it in the love of my wife Beth.

If we could express our Love fully,
it might overwhelm us.
It is too great, too terrible for words—
a Thing of Awe.
And so Love finds expression in small things—
a tender smile,
a warm hug,
an act of contrition or forgiveness,
an unresolved tear.

And yet Love is more real than any earthly bond,
even gravity,
for only Love allows us to be wholly unique, yet holy One.

So let us be content, then, at least for now,
with these small expressions of Love—
a Love so profound that to acknowledge it fully
would be to wrench ourselves from this earth to the highest heaven ...
and yet we still have so much work to do here, however hole-y,
oh, my sweet darling dear!

Sip from the teacup,
the tide lies beyond you;
stick a toe in Love's ocean,
lest Heaven abscond you!

The Search

To know your own worth
search all over the earth —
where else is there passion
like yours, or compassion,
or a longing for perfection?
Or, not finding it, dejection?

I know where to start —
for your heart is God's heart.
When all others agree
this hatred-scarred earth
will finally be
heavenly.

Love's Exemplar

Life here on earth is hard, it's true,
from our harrowing birth till the day life is through
for it's here angels fashion
hearts filled with compassion,
and kindest of angels is you!

My Angel

O little fallen wren,
who so valiantly struggled to fly—
how could my prayers not avail
your efforts? *Why, O, why?*
My starling, flown off to the stars,
my turtle, my sweet, my dove,
my Angel, sweet Spirit of Love!—
watch over me now, from above.
We struggle, who live here on earth;
so remember my prayers for you.
And now, because you're so dear—
please remember—my love was true
and grant me my cherished thought—
that no sparrow shall fall here, uncaught.

Amen

Your Heart's Rose (I)

The rose within its whorls contains
perfumes and lustres—mysteries
redolent of love and its verities.

Your heart within its whorls remains
secluded and lovely, tender and warm—
more exquisite treasure, without barbarous thorns.

Your Heart's Rose (II)

I have seen your heart flower
in its triumphant hour
to a rose of such beauty
it out-splendors the ruby.

Beth's Advice to a Slowly Awakening World

This is the day of new beginnings —
act only in love; cast aside hatred's sinnings!

My Epitaph

I lived and strove with all my might to make
my name my own, and hers, for Beth's sweet sake.
Now, if we lie together or apart,
always, eternally, she has my heart.

Amen

Requiem: Remember My Laughter

... if some day I am absent, and loss
collects in the wound, or floods the ravine,
or blocks out the sun like a thick Spanish moss
webbing over the canopy of heaven ...
then darling, remember my Laughter, and smile
at my sillier poems and their tenderer moments
and remember the wisdom of Will, who said I'll
be one of those Poets more immortal than comets
who flashed through the heavens to leave a Wild Mark
on the incoherent dark.

After the Deluge (I)

After the flood let me never forget
the anguished cries of the plangent
banshees,
the terrified geese,
the immense seas
turgid with death
or the way these
hardened eyes breasted tears.

After the flood let me never forget
the happiest thought of my fifty-two years—
your beatific face
once again gracing my threshold.

After the flood let me always remember
and never forget—the sweetness, the light,
the immaculate grace of your Presence
almost lost to the Vortex and Night.

After the Deluge (II)

She was kinder than light
to an up-reaching flower
and sweeter than rain
to the bees in their bower
where anemones blush
at the affections they shower,
and love's shocking power.

She shocked me to life,
but soon left me to wither.
I was listless without her,
nor could I be with her.
I fell under the spell
of her absence's power.
in that calamitous hour.

Like blithe showers that fled
repealing spring's sweetness;
like suns' warming rays sped
away with such fleetness ...
she has vanished, with my heart—
alas, our completeness!
I now wilt in pale beams
of her occult remembrance.

My Eve (I)

On the holy mountain of Zion
let the lamb lie down with the lion
and let my Eve befriend them
and—oh, so tenderly—tend them,
as they nuzzle and snuggle her feet,
when creation is complete.

When creation is complete
and they nuzzle and snuggle her feet
—the gentle lamb and the mighty lion
on the holy mountain of Zion—
even the Angels shall believe
in the love of my lovely Eve.

My Eve (II)

In my dreams I see the gentle does
gather 'round, for each one knows
the tender hands of love are yours,
and gentleness your guiding force,
as theirs.

And soon the shy fawns also come,
beguiled by kindness—till the sum
of amiable creatures is compounded
and even the heavens sing astounded
immaculate prayers.

Look! Now, from afar, a sweet black form
runs to your arms! The angels, charmed,
beam as their Mentor's reunited
with my sweet Eve who claps, delighted,
done with all cares.

Love
for Beth, possibly channeled from her Father?

to use the word seems sacrilege
for any mortal man,
after seeing *how* You love,
as only angels can

but half of loving is the Other—
their dreams and strong desire
to have You hale and whole again,
your sparkling eyes afire

you were my Glory, and still are,
and evermore shall be
but please be mindful of your flesh,
this side of Eternity ...

Enigma (II)

My darling, my gorgeous one,
you have a good, great and wonderful heart.

And, while I hate to see you in such pain,
it pains me all the more to hear you suggest, even for a second,
that you are somehow "unworthy"
because the circumstances of life on a very difficult planet
sometimes lead to mistakes.

Everyone makes mistakes
(all we can do is overcome them)
and how can anyone be "unworthy" of love
or of any good thing,
especially an Angel like you!

I hope that very soon—nay, today!—you will see yourself
in the proper, appreciative viewpoint
of my eyes,
which will be to see yourself as you truly are:
completely and utterly amazing,
a Gem without flaw
needing only the proper setting
to astound even the myopic.

O, when will you see yourself as you truly are,
my darling, my gorgeous one,
my embodiment of Love,
my most precious Enigma!

Note: The Roman numeral for two consists of two independent I's standing together as one.

Mother's Smile

There never was a fonder smile
than mother's smile, no softer touch
than mother's touch. So sleep awhile
and know she loves you more than "much."
So more than "much," much more than "all."
Though tender words, these do not speak
of love at all, nor how we fall
and mother's there, nor how we reach
from nightmares in the ticking night
and she is there to hold us tight.

There never was a stronger back
than father's back, that held our weight
and lifted us, when we were small,
and bore us till we reached the gate,
then held our hands that first bright mile
till we could run, and did, and flew.
But, oh, a mother's tender smile
will leap and follow after you!

The Desk
for Jeremy

There is a child I used to know
who sat, perhaps, at this same desk
where you sit now, and made a mess
of things sometimes.
I wonder how
he learned at all ...

He saw T-Rexes down the hall
and dreamed of trains and cars and wrecks.
He dribbled phantom basketballs,
shot spitwads at his schoolmates' necks.

He played with pasty Elmer's glue
(and sometimes got the glue on you!).
He earned the nickname—"teacher's PEST."

His mother had to come to school
because he broke the golden rule.
He dreaded each and every test.

But something happened in the fall—
he grew up big and straight and tall,
and now his desk is far too small;
so you can have it.

One thing, though—
one swirling autumn, one bright snow,
one gooey tube of Elmer's glue ...
and you'll outgrow this old desk, too.

Reflex
for Jeremy

Some intuition of her despair
for her lost brood,
as though a last fragment of song
torn from her flat breast,
touched me there ...

I felt, unable to hear
through the bright glass,
the being within her melt
as her unseemly tirade
left a feather or two
adrift on the wind-ruffled air.

Where she will go,
how we all err,
why we all fear
for the lives of our children,
I cannot pretend to know.

But, O!,
how the unappeased glare
of omnivorous sun
over crimson-flecked snow
makes me wish you were here.

Precipice
for Jeremy

They will teach you to scoff at love
from the highest, windiest precipice of reason.

Do not believe them.

There is no place safe for you to fall
save into the arms of love.

Success
for Jeremy

We need our children to keep us humble
between toast and marmalade;

there is no time for a ticker-tape parade
before bed, no award, no bright statuette

to be delivered for mending skinned knees,
no wild bursts of approval for shoveling snow.

A kiss is the only approval they show;
to leave us—the first great success they achieve.

Love's Extreme Unction

Lines composed during Jeremy's first high school football game (he played tuba), while watching Beth watch him.

Within the intimate chapels of her eyes—
devotions, meditations, reverence.
I find in them Love's very residence
and hearing the ardent rapture of her sighs
I prophesy beatitudes to come,
when Love like hers commands us, "All be One!"

Within her inner sanctum there is bliss
unaccountable as angels' bliss above.
So a man might find his knees, might speak of love
as vainly as when Cupid's arrows miss—
for to speak of "love" is merely to profane
the sacredness and blessedness of rain:
this rain of tears of pleasure, and of pain,
Love's unction and communion and refrain.

Boundless
for Jeremy

Every day we whittle away at the essential solidity of him,
and every day a new sharp feature emerges: a feature we'll
spend creative years: planing, smoothing, refining,
trying to find some new Bust of Apollo, or Thinker.
And if each new day a little of the boisterous air of youth is
deflated in him; if the hours of small pleasures spent chasing
daffodils in the outfield *as the singles become doubles, become
triples, become unconscionable errors, become victories lost,
become lives wasted beyond all possible hope of repair ...*
If who he was becomes increasingly vague—like a white
balloon careening into clouds; like a child striding away aggressively toward manhood, hitching an impressive rucksack over sagging, sloping shoulders, shifting its vaudevillian
burden back and forth, then pausing to look back at us with
an almost comical longing ...
If what he wants is only to be held a little longer against a
forgiving bosom; to chase after daffodils in the outfield regardless of scores; to sail away like a balloon on a firm string,
always sure to return when the line tautens, till he looks
down upon us from some removed height we cannot quite
see, bursting into tears over us ...
What, then, of our aspirations for him, if he cannot breathe,
cannot rise enough to contemplate the earth with his own
vision,
unencumbered, but never untethered, never forsaken ...
if he cannot grow brightly, steadily, into himself—flying
wildly beyond us?

Lullaby
for Jeremy

Cherubic laugh; sly, impish grin.
Angelic face; wild chimp within.

It does not matter; sleep awhile
as soft mirth tickles forth a smile.

Gray moths will hum a lullaby
of feathery wings, then you and I

will wake together, by and by.

*

Life is not long; those days are best
spent snuggled to a loving breast.

The earth will wait; a sun-filled sky
will bronze lean muscle, by and by.

Soon you will sing, with watchful eye.
But sleep here, now, for you and I

know nothing but this lullaby.

A True Story
for Jeremy

Jeremy hit the ball today,
over the fence and far away.
So very, very far away
a neighbor had to toss it back.
(She thought it was an air attack!)

Jeremy hit the ball so hard
it flew across his neighbor's yard.
So very hard across her yard
the bat that boomed a mighty "THWACK!"
now shows an eensy-teensy crack.

Always
for Jeremy

Know in your heart that I love you as no other,
and that my love is eternal.
I keep the record of your hopes and dreams
in my heart like a journal,
and there are pages for you there that no one else can fill:
none one else, ever.
And there is a tie between us, more than blood,
that no one else can sever.

And if we're ever parted,
please don't be broken-hearted;
until we meet again on the far side of forever
and walk among those storied shining ways,
should we, for any reason, be apart,
still, I am with you ... always.

Hushed, Yet Melodic
for Jeremy

Hushed, yet melodic, the hills and the valleys
sleep unaware of the nightingale's call,
but all of the stars are listening,
glistening ...
this is their night, the first night of fall.

Son, tonight, a woman awaits you;
she is more vibrant, more lovely than spring.
She'll meet you in moonlight, soft and warm,
all alone ...
then you'll know why the nightingale sings.

Just yesterday the stars were afire;
then how desire flashed through my veins.
But now I am older; night has come,
I'm alone ...
for you I will sing as the nightingale sings.

Passages on Fatherhood
for Jeremy

He is my treasure,
and by his happiness I measure
my own worth.

Four years old,
with all the earth's diamonds and gold
bejeweled in his soul.

The wisdoms of ages
and prophets and mages
and doddering sages

is useless
unless
it encompasses this.

The Watch
for Jeremy

I have come to watch my young son,
his blonde ringlets damp with sleep ...
and what I know is that he loves me
beyond all earthly understanding,
that his life is like clay in my unskilled hands.

And I marvel this bright ore does not keep—
unrestricted in form, more content than shape,
but seeking a form to become, to express
something of itself to this wilderness
of eyes watching and waiting.

What do I know of his wonder, his awe?
To his future I will matter less and less,
but in this moment, as he is my world, I am his,
and I stand, not understanding, but knowing—
in this vast pageant of stars, he is more than unique.

There will never be another moment like this.
Studiously quiet, I stroke his fine hair
which will darken and coarsen and straighten with time.
He is all I bequeath of myself to this earth.
His fingers curl around mine in his sleep ...
I leave him to dreams—calm, untroubled and deep.

To My Child, Unborn
for Jeremy

How many were the nights, enchanted
with despair and longing, when dreams recanted
returned with a restless yearning,
and the pale stars, burning,
cried out at me to remember
one night ... long ere the September
night when you were conceived.

Oh, then, if only I might have believed
that the future held such mystery
as you, my child, come unbidden to me
and to your mother,
come to us out of a realm of wonder,
come to us out of a faery clime ...

If only then, in that distant time,
I had known that this day were coming,
I might not have despaired at the raindrops drumming
their anthems of loneliness against shuttered panes;
I might not have considered my doubts and my pains
so carefully, so cheerlessly, as if they were never-ending.
If only then, with the starlight mending
the shadows that formed
in the bowels of those nights, in the gussets of storms
that threatened till dawn as though never leaving,
I might not have spent those long nights grieving,
lamenting my loneliness, cursing the sun
for its late arrival. Now, a coming dawn
brings you unto us, and you shall be ours,
as welcome as ever the moon or the stars
or the glorious sun when the nighttime is through
and the earth is enchanted with skies turning blue.

Transition
for Jeremy

With his cocklebur hugs
and his wet, clinging kisses
like a damp, trembling thistle
catching, thwarting my legs—
he reminds me that life begins
with the possibility of rapture.

What Does It Mean?
for Jeremy

His little hand, held fast in mine.
What does it mean? What does it mean?
If he were not here, the sun would not shine,
nor the grass grow half as green.
What does it mean?

His arms around my neck, his cheek
so warm against my own.
What does it mean?

If life's a garden, he's the fairest
flower ever sown,
the sweetest ever seen.
What does it mean?

And when he whispers sweet and low,
"What does it mean?"
It means, my son, I love you so.
Sometimes that's all we need to know.

With a Child's Wonder
for Jeremy

With a child's wonder,
pausing to ponder
a puddle of water,
but just for a moment,
needing no comment
but bright eyes
and a wordless cry,
he launches himself to fly ...

then my two-year-old lands
on his feet and his hands
and water falls all around.

(From the impact and sound
you'd have thought that he'd drowned,
but the puddle was two inches deep.)

Later that evening, as he lay fast asleep
in that dreamland where two-year-olds wander,
I watched him awhile and smilingly pondered
with a father's wonder.

About Michael R. Burch

Michael R. Burch has been published widely around the globe. He has had articles, essays and/or letters published in *TIME, USA Today, The Hindu, The Washington Post, The Tennessean,* and other major magazines and newspapers. He also writes a weekly column for the *Nashville City Paper.* His poetry has appeared in hundreds of literary journals, including *The Lyric, Light Quarterly, Measure, Poet Lore, Romantics Quarterly, The New Formalist, Trinacria* and *Writer's Digest – The Year's Best Writing.* According to Google's search term rankings, through his literary website *The HyperTexts* he is a leading online publisher of poetry about the Holocaust, the Nakba, Hiroshima, Darfur, the Trail of Tears, and other similar events.

He lives in Nashville, Tennessee, with his lovely wife Beth, his handsome son Jeremy, and six outrageously spoiled puppies.

www.ingramcontent.com/pod-product-compliance
Lightning Source LLC
Chambersburg PA
CBHW070517100426
42743CB00010B/1848